FORWARD

One of the more important functions of any police agency is the processing of fingerprint images and cards, whether it deals with criminal or applicant contributors. At no time is there a higher sense of frustration than when the fingerprints obtained and submitted to the FBI have been returned because of missing, illegible or incomplete data or the fingerprint images are of such poor quality that they cannot be processed.

This guide has been prepared to assist local, state and federal law enforcement governmental agencies and authorized applicant contributors in the preparation of the FBI Criminal Fingerprint Card (Form FD-249), FBI Applicant Fingerprint Card (Form FD-258), FBI Palmprint cards (Forms FD 884 and 884a), FBI Final Disposition Report (R-84), and FBI Flash/Cancellation Notice (Form I-12). Included are examples and instructions that will identify the correct manner in which data is to be recorded on the fingerprint cards including code tables for entry of personal descriptors. Also included are instructions on how to obtain legible fingerprints.

This guide has been designed to assist you and your department in meeting its goal of receiving prompt identification services and results. It will help you report correct and complete information in the standardized manner. This enables the FBI to process the fingerprint cards and associated documents more promptly and with less chance of error.

The Guidelines for Preparation of Fingerprints and Associated Criminal History Information should also be applied to electronic fingerprint submissions. For additional specifications and requirements for submitting electronic fingerprint submissions, please refer to the *Criminal Justice Information Services Electronic Biometric Transmission Specifications (EBTS) Manual*. For additional guidance in submitting Criminal History Information please refer to the *Interstate Criminal History Specifications Guide*.

Criminal Justice Information Services Division
Mission Statement

TO REDUCE TERRORIST AND CRIMINAL ACTIVITY by maximizing the ability to provide timely and relevant criminal justice information to the FBI and to qualified law enforcement, criminal justice, civilian, academic, employment, and licensing agencies concerning individual, stolen property, criminal organization and activities and other law enforcement-related data.

INTRODUCTION

PROCESSING DELAYS AND/OR REJECTION
OF FINGERPRINT SUBMISSIONS

The Criminal Justice Information Services (CJIS) Division provides identification services based on fingerprint submissions. To better serve the criminal justice community, the CJIS Division attempts to prevent delays in processing and/or rejections of fingerprints by addressing problems commonly encountered.

Paper fingerprint submission must meet specific criteria to be converted into an electronic format and processed by the Integrated Automated Fingerprint Identification System (IAFIS). The following may cause a rejection or delay in processing:

- Low quality print by dot matrix printers
- Poor penmanship
- Use of highlighter in entry block
- Entry not within boundaries of entry block
- Labels applied to "Leave Blank" areas
- Submission on non-standard fingerprint card
- Use of pencil or ink other than blue or black

Paper or electronic fingerprint submissions may also be rejected for the following reasons:

- Missing or invalid required data (i.e. date of birth)
- Descriptive data not complete (i.e. name not shown at top of card)
- Charge is not complete
- Missing Originating Agency Identifier
- No attempt to print deformed or scarred fingers in both rolled and plain impression blocks
- More than one fingerprint impression per block (It must be indicated if an individual has extra digits, split thumbs or webbed fingers)
- Fingerprints not properly rolled or poor quality
- Fingerprints on back of fingerprint card
- Fingerprints out of sequence
- Finger(s) missing due to amputation and not noted as "AMP" or "XX" in fingerprint block
- Missing fingerprints with no reason given including the plain "flat" impressions
- More than two FBI approved "Retabs" per fingerprint block on a paper fingerprint card

TABLE OF CONTENTS

REQUIRED FIELDS – CRIMINAL FINGERPRINT CARD

If any of the Required Fields are left blank, the card will be rejected without further processing unless there is a quoted FBI number.

Every effort should be made to enter the appropriate data in all fields (blocks) as shown on the fingerprint card.

Name (NAM)

Originating Agency Identifier (ORI) Number

Date of Birth (DOB)

Sex (SEX)

Charge

Fingerprint Impressions

All data entered on fingerprint cards must be typewritten or legibly printed, utilizing black or blue ink and must not exceed the boundaries of the designated field (block).

DATA ENTERED ON CRIMINAL FINGERPRINT CARDS

See figures 1 and 2 on pages 9 and 10 for a Criminal fingerprint Card (FD–249) example.

Data fields preceded by an asterisk (*) must be completed in order for a fingerprint card to be processed by the FBI. However, all data fields are important and should be completed if the information is known. Also, the *National Crime Information Center (NCIC) Code Manual* can be used as a reference for codes of various fields.

1.   *Name (NAM) Block

Enter the name obtained from the subject in this field. Abbreviations are not to be used for any part of the name. The format is last name followed by a comma (,) and first and middle names. Suffixes denoting seniority (Jr., Sr., III, etc.) should follow the middle or first name. Do not obstruct this area by using stamps, labels, holes or staples where the name has been printed.

2.   Signature of Person Fingerprinted Block

Obtain the signature of the person being fingerprinted, in ink.

3.   Social Security Number (SOC) Block

Enter the subject's Social Security number, if known. Additional Social Security numbers used by the subject may be entered in the "Additional Information/Basis for Caution" block #34 on the reverse side of the fingerprint card.

4.   Alias/Maiden Name (AKA) Block

Enter other names used by the subject that are different than the name entered in "NAM" block #1 including the signature name, using the same format (i.e. LAST, FIRST, MIDDLE, SUFFIX).

If more space is needed, enter additional aliases in the "Additional Information/Basis for Caution" block #34 on the reverse side of the fingerprint card. Maiden names and all previous married names of females should be entered in the alias field, if known.

5.   FBI Number (FBI) Block

Enter the assigned FBI number for the subject, if known.

6. **State Identification Number (SID) Block**

Enter the SID number when known. Enter SID number with no more than ten (10) alphanumeric characters, which includes the state abbreviation (i.e. NYXXXXXXXX). If labels are used for the SID numbers, ensure the label used is an appropriate size for the SID block. **When the SID number is missing from a National Fingerprint File (NFF) participant, the card will be rejected.**

7. ***Date of Birth (DOB) Block**

Enter the DOB in month, day and year format (i.e. MM/DD/YYYY). If a complete DOB is not known, enter the approximate age followed by the statement "YEARS OF AGE". **Fingerprint cards of persons 99 years old or older are not processed by the FBI; they will be rejected immediately.**

> NOTE: IF THE **DOB** BLOCK IS BLANK AND THE CARD DOES NOT HAVE AN FBI NUMBER QUOTED, THE CARD WILL BE RETURNED TO THE STATE BUREAU OR SUBMITTING AGENCY WITHOUT BEING PROCESSED.

8. ***Sex (SEX) Block**

Sex must be indicated by either "F" (female) or "M" (male). See Sex Code Table on page 37 for additional codes.

9. **Race (RAC) Block**

Race must be indicated by using the race code table on page 39.

10. **Height (HGT) Block**

Height must be expressed in feet and inches. Fractions of an inch should be rounded off to the nearest inch. Inches less than ten should be preceded by a zero. For example, five feet four inches should be submitted as "504" and six feet even should be submitted as "600".

11. **Weight (WGT) Block**

Weight must be expressed in pounds. Fractions of pounds should be rounded off to the nearest pound.

12. **Eye (EYE) Block**

Indicate eye color by entering one of the three-character codes from the Eye Code Chart on page 37.

13. Hair (HAI) Block

Indicate hair color by entering one of the three-character codes from the Hair Code Chart on page 38.

14. *Fingerprint Impression Blocks (Individual and Simultaneous)

It is very important that care be taken to roll the fingers from nail to nail when recording individual finger impressions. This will help ensure legibility. Roll the prints in the correct sequence code (note the right and left hand designations in the finger blocks) and obtain simultaneous plain "flat" impressions at 45 degree angles that do not extend up into the rolled impressions. Indicate amputated fingers, tip-amputated, transplanted toes/fingers, missing at birth, deformed, bandaged, scars, etc., in the appropriate finger block(s).

> **NOTE:** FBI APPROVED "RETABS" CAN BE APPLIED TO ALL FINGER BLOCKS ON A FINGERPRINT CARD IF NECESSARY, WITH A LIMIT OF TWO (2) "RETABS" PER BLOCK.

15. Juvenile Fingerprint Block

If the subject is charged as an adult, this should be indicated by checking both boxes. Juvenile fingerprint cards will be accepted and retained provided the card contains criterion charges and there is no indication that the card should be returned to your agency.

16. Date of Arrest (DOA) Block

Enter the date the subject was arrested in month, day, year format (i.e. MM/DD/YYYY). If the contributor is a prison/jail, enter the date received.

17. Originating Agency Identifier (ORI) Block

If the ORI number is not preprinted by the FBI, enter your ORI number, agency name, city and state. Each agency has its own unique ORI number. If you do not have an ORI number, contact your National Crime Information Center (NCIC) Control Terminal Officer (CTO), and an ORI number will be assigned to your agency. Federal agencies should contact their Federal Service Coordinator to obtain an ORI number.

If a **reply** is desired, check the **"YES"** block. A reply will be sent only if this block is checked.

IMPORTANT:
        **NEVER BORROW PREPRINTED FINGERPRINT CARDS FROM
        OR LOAN YOUR PREPRINTED FINGERPRINT CARDS TO
        OTHER AGENCIES.**

18.   **Send Copy To (SCT) Block**

Indicate the ORI number(s) of additional agencies to whom you want copies of the response sent. Do not enter your agency's ORI number in this block.

19.   **Date of Offense (DOO) Block**

Enter the date the offense was committed in month, day, and year format (i.e. MM/DD/YYYY). Leave blank if the date of offense is unknown.

20.   **Place of Birth (POB) Block (State or Country)**

Enter the state, territorial possession, province (Canadian), or country of birth. Use the correct abbreviation for foreign countries or correctly spell the name of the country. A list of approved abbreviations can be found in the *NCIC Code Manual*. **Do no list a county as a POB.**

21.   **Country of Citizenship (CTZ) Block**

Enter "U.S." if subject is a citizen of the United States; otherwise, enter appropriate country. Use the correct abbreviation for foreign countries or correctly spell the name of the country. A list of approved abbreviations can be found in the *NCIC Code Manual*. **"YES"** or **"NO"** responses are not acceptable.

22.   **Miscellaneous Number (MNU) Block**

The MNU is an identifying number associated with the subject such as a U.S. Military Service Number, Passport Number, etc. Enter the appropriate code from the MNU chart on page 40, a hyphen (-), then the MNU.

23.   **Scars, Marks, Tattoos (SMT) and Amputations Block**

Enter any scars, marks, tattoos, discolorations, moles, missing or artificial body parts, deformities, piercings, needle marks, transplanted toes/fingers, and/or amputations. Finger, hand, and arm amputations should also be noted in appropriate finger block(s) on the front side of the card. A list of approved abbreviations can be found in the *NCIC Code Manual*.

24. Residence/Complete Address (ADR) Block

Enter complete residential address and zip code obtained from the subject's identification.

25. Official Taking Fingerprints Block

Enter the name or number of the official taking fingerprints.

26. Local Agency Identification/Reference (LIR) Number Block

Enter your agency's identification or case number for the subject. If unavailable, leave this block blank.

27. Photo and Palmprints Block

Check "YES" to indicate if a photo and/or palmprints are available. If unavailable, leave this block blank.

28. Employer Block

If the subject's employer is the U.S. Government, indicate a specific agency. If the subject's employer is the military, list the specific branch of service and serial number. Otherwise, indicate the company or agency where the subject is employed.

29. Occupation block

Indicate occupation, if available.

30. *Charge/Citation Block

Enter the charge(s) in literal terms (i.e. murder, rape, robbery, assault, etc.). Please note the numeric four digit NCIC Codes should not be used. Each charge block entry can be up to 300 characters. While abbreviations should not routinely be used, only easily understood abbreviations should be submitted when charge information needs to be shortened.

State or local citation numbers may be listed but the literal should also be listed. If federal citation numbers are listed, a literal should be listed also. Charge literals are important for those using the Criminal History Record for licensing, employment suitability determination and agencies that do not have access to all citation numbers that may be used.

Place one charge in each space provided. If there are more than three charges, continue numbering and place additional charge(s) in the "Additional Information/Basis for Caution" block #34.

EXCEPTION: If a subject is arrested on multiple charges and there is one final disposition that pertains to all charges, each charge may be listed in the same block with the disposition in the corresponding block across from it.

31. Disposition Block

If available, enter the disposition data including the sentence date for each corresponding charge. Indicate the type of sentence imposed if applicable (i.e. consecutive, concurrent, probation, etc.). Number each disposition to correspond with the appropriate charge. If the subject was convicted or plead guilty to a lesser charge, include the modification with the disposition. **If a single disposition applies to all charges listed, please indicate**. If the disposition is not available at the time fingerprinted, submit an update on Form R-84. It is not necessary to list **"Disposition not available", "Not yet disposed", or any similar phrase.** If more space is needed, continue numbering and place additional dispositional data in the "Additional" block #32, (Dispositions).

32. Additional Block (Charges)

Enter additional charges when there are more than three and number each one. If more space is needed, continue numbering and place additional charge(s) in the "Additional Information/Basis for Caution" block #34.

33. Additional Block (Disposition)

If available, enter the final dispositional data for each corresponding charge when there are more than three and number each one. If more space is needed, continue numbering and place additional dispositional data in the "State Bureau Stamp" block #35.

34. Additional Information/Basis for Caution Block

Enter additional or multi-informational data that did not fit in the blocks provided (i.e. Additional DOB's, or Additional SOC's). In addition this block also provides reason for caution. Information which indicates a condition that could be expected to continue when dealing with the subject (i.e. escape risk, armed and dangerous, martial arts, etc.) should be entered.

35.   **State Bureau Stamp Block**

When a card is from a single source state participant, and the card does not reflect your state bureau identification stamp, **the card will be immediately returned to the state bureau/submitting agency**. Check with your state repository to determine if you are a single source state.

NOTE:	AT THIS POINT, A QUALITY REVIEW OF ARREST AND PERSONAL DESCRIPTOR DATA IS EXTREMELY IMPORTANT. THIS STEP CAN IMPROVE THE QUALITY OF THE SUBMISSION AND HELP ELIMINATE IMMEDIATE REJECTS (CARDS RETURNED BY THE FBI WITHOUT ANY PROCESSING.

STATE USAGE

NEF SECOND

SUBMISSION	APPROXIMATE CLASS	AMPUTATION	SCAR

DATE USAGE

LAST NAME, FIRST NAME, MIDDLE NAME, SUFFIX

1

SIGNATURE OF PERSON FINGERPRINTED

2

SOCIAL SECURITY NO.

3

LEAVE BLANK

ALIASES/MAIDEN
LAST NAME, FIRST NAME, MIDDLE NAME, SUFFIX

4

FBI NO.	STATE IDENTIFICATION NO.	DATE OF BIRTH MM DD YY	SEX	RACE	HEIGHT	WEIGHT	EYES	HAIR
5	6	7	8	9	10	11	12	13

14

1. R. THUMB	2. R. INDEX	3. R. MIDDLE	4. R. RING	5. R. LITTLE

6. L. THUMB	7. L. INDEX	8. L. MIDDLE	9. L. RING	10. L. LITTLE

LEFT FOUR FINGERS TAKEN SIMULTANEOUSLY	L. THUMB	R. THUMB	RIGHT FOUR FINGERS TAKEN SIMULTANEOUSLY

FEDERAL BUREAU OF INVESTIGATION, UNITED STATES DEPARTMENT OF JUSTICE
CRIMINAL JUSTICE INFORMATION SERVICES DIVISION, CLARKSBURG, WV 26306

PRIVACY ACT OF 1974 (PL 93-579) REQUIRES THAT FEDERAL, STATE, OR LOCAL AGENCIES INFORM INDIVIDUALS WHOSE SOCIAL SECURITY NUMBER IS REQUESTED WHETHER SUCH DISCLOSURE IS MANDATORY OR VOLUNTARY, BASIS OF AUTHORITY FOR SUCH SOLICITATION, AND USES WHICH WILL BE MADE OF IT.

JUVENILE FINGERPRINT	DATE OF ARREST	ORI
SUBMISSION YES ☐ 15	16 MM DD YY	CONTRIBUTOR 17
TREAT AS ADULT YES ☐		ADDRESS
		REPLY YES ☐ DESIRED?

SEND COPY TO: (ENTER ORI) 18	DATE OF OFFENSE 19 MM DD YY	PLACE OF BIRTH (STATE OR COUNTRY) 20	COUNTRY OF CITIZENSHIP 21

MISCELLANEOUS NUMBERS 22	SCARS, MARKS, TATTOOS, AND AMPUTATIONS 23		
	RESIDENCE/COMPLETE ADDRESS 24	CITY	STATE

OFFICIAL TAKING FINGERPRINTS (NAME OR NUMBER) 25	LOCAL IDENTIFICATION/REFERENCE 26	PHOTO AVAILABLE? YES ☐
		PALM PRINTS TAKEN? 27 YES ☐

EMPLOYER IF U.S. GOVERNMENT, INDICATE SPECIFIC AGENCY. IF MILITARY, LIST BRANCH OF SERVICE AND SERIAL NO. 28	OCCUPATION 29

CHARGE/CITATION 1. 30	DISPOSITION 1. 31
2.	2.
3.	3.
ADDITIONAL 32	ADDITIONAL 33
ADDITIONAL INFORMATION/BASIS FOR CAUTION 34	STATE BUREAU STAMP 35

FD-249 (Rev. 5-11-99) 349-448/80048

REQUIRED FIELDS – CIVIL FINGERPRINT CARDS

If any of the required fields are left blank, the fingerprint card will be rejected without further processing unless there is a quoted FBI Number.

Every effort should be made to enter the appropriate data in all fields (blocks) as shown on the fingerprint card.

Name (NAM)

Originating Agency Identifier (ORI)

Date of Birth (DOB)

Sex (SEX)

Fingerprint Impressions

Reason Fingerprinted

All data entered on fingerprint cards must be typewritten or legibly printed, utilizing black or blue ink and must not exceed the boundaries of the designated field (block).

DATA ENTERED ON CIVIL FINGERPRINT CARDS

See figure 3 on page 17 for an example of a Civil Fingerprint Card (FD-258)

Data fields preceded by an asterisk (*) must be completed in order for a fingerprint card to be processed by the FBI. However, all data fields are important and should be completed if the information is known. Also, the *National Crime Information Center (NCIC) Code Manual* can be used as a reference for codes of various fields.

1. ***Name (NAM) Block**

    Enter the name obtained from the subject in this field. Abbreviations are not to be used for any part of the name. This format is last name followed by a comma (,) first and middle name, if any. Suffixes denoting seniority (i.e. Jr., Sr., III, etc.) should follow the middle or first name. Do not obstruct this area by using stamps, labels, holes or staples where the name has been printed.

2. **Signature and residence of Person Fingerprinted Block**

    Obtain the signature of the person being fingerprinted, in ink. Also, enter the residential address of the person being fingerprinted.

3. **Aliases (AKA) Block**

    Enter other names used by the subject that are different than the name entered in the "NAM" block #1. Also list the signature name as an AKA if different than the name that appears in the "NAM" block. Maiden names and all previous married names of females should be entered in the AKA field, if known.

4. ***Originating Agency Identifier (ORI) Block**

    If the ORI number is not preprinted by the FBI, enter the ORI number, agency name, city and state. Each agency is assigned its own unique ORI number. If you do not have an ORI number, you can contact your NCIC Control Terminal Officer (CTO), and an ORI number will be assigned to your agency. Federal agencies should contact their Federal Service Coordinator to obtain an ORI number.

IMPORTANT:

NEVER BORROW PREPRINTED FINGERPRINT CARDS FROM OR LOAN PREPRINTED FINGERPRINT CARDS TO OTHER AGENCIES.

5.   ***Date of Birth (DOB) Block**

Enter the DOB in month, day, year format (i.e. MM/DD/YYYY). If a complete DOB is not known, enter approximate age followed by the statement "YEARS OF AGE". **Fingerprint cards of person 99 years old or older are not processed by the FBI; they will be rejected.**

NOTE: IF THE DOB BLOCK IS BLANK AND THE CARD DOES NOT HAVE AN FBI NUMBER QUOTED, THE CARD WILL BE RETURNED TO THE STATE BUREAU OR SUBMITTING AGENCY WITHOUT BEING PROCESSED.

---

6.   **Citizenship (CTZ) Block**

Enter "U.S." if the subject is a citizen of the United States; otherwise, enter the appropriate country. Use the correct abbreviation for foreign countries or correctly spell the name of the country. A list of approved abbreviations can be found in the *NCIC Code Manual*. **"YES"** or **"NO"** responses are not acceptable.

7.   ***Sex (SEX) Block**

Sex must be indicated by either **"F"** (female) or **"M"** (male). See Sex Code Table on page 37 for additional codes.

8.   **Race (RAC) Block**

Race must be indicated by using the Race Code decision chart on page 39.

NOTE: ADDITIONAL EXPLANATIONS OF SEX AND RACE CODES ARE LISTED ON PAGE 37AND 39.

---

9.   **Height (HGT) Block**

Height must be expressed in feet and inches. Fractions of an inch should be rounded off to the nearest inch. Inches less than ten should be preceded by a zero. For example, five feet four inches should be submitted as "504" and six feet even would be "600".

10.   **Weight (WGT) Block**

Weight must be expressed in pounds. Fractions of a pound should be rounded off to the nearest pound.

11. **Eye (EYE) Color Block**

Indicate eye color by entering one of the codes from the eye color decision chart on page 37.

12. **Hair (HAI) color Block**

Indicate hair color by entering one of the codes from the hair color decision chart on page 38.

13. **Place of Birth (POB) Block**

Enter the subject's state, territorial possession, province (Canadian), or country of birth. Use the correct abbreviation for foreign countries or correctly spell the name of the country. A list of approved abbreviations can be found in the *NCIC Code Manual*. **Do not list a county as a POB.**

14. **Originating Case Agency/Local Agency Identification Reference (OCA/LIR) Block**

Enter your agency's identification or case number for the subject. The OCA must not exceed twenty (20) alphanumeric characters.

15. **FBI Number (FBI) Block**

Enter the assigned FBI Number for the subject, if known.

16. **Armed Forces Number (MNU) Block**

Enter Armed Forces number, if known.

17. **Social Security Number (SOC) Block**

Enter the subject's Social Security number, if known.

18. **Miscellaneous Number (MNU) Block**

The MNU is an identifying number associated with the subject such as U.S. Military Service Number, Passport Number, etc. Enter the MNU and indicate the description according to the decision chart on page 40.

19. **Date Fingerprinted Block**

Enter the date the subject was fingerprinted in month, day, year format (i.e. MM/DD/YYYY).

20. **Signature of Official Taking Fingerprints Block**

Enter the signature or name of the official taking fingerprints. Also list the official's ID number if applicable.

21. **Employer and Address Block**

Enter the subject's potential employer and address of that employer.

22. **Reason Fingerprinted Block**

Miscellaneous Applicant: Fingerprint cards are submitted when a person is applying for law enforcement/criminal justice background checks. Clearly state the position and or agency as applicable such as: Law Enforcement Officer, Corrections Officer, NCIC Terminal Operator, etc.

Applicant User Fee: Fingerprint cards are submitted when a person is applying for a non-law enforcement position and needs a background check completed as part of the hiring/licensing process (i.e. teacher, day care provider, school bus driver, racing commission, liquor license, etc.). Non-Federal Applicant User Fee fingerprint card submissions are governed by state statutes. A statute must be included in the Reason Fingerprinted block and coincide with the literal (i.e. Pharmacists B&PC 4345, Notaries Public Gov C 82141, AS 13.08.015 Permit for School Bus Driver).

23. ***Fingerprint Impressions Block (Individual & Simultaneous)**

Care should be taken to roll the fingers from nail to nail when taking the individual finger impressions. This will help ensure legibility. Roll the prints in the correct sequence code (note the right and left hand designations in the finger blocks) and obtain simultaneous plain "flat" impressions at 45 degree angles that do not extend up into the rolled impressions. Indicate amputated fingers, tip-amputated, transplanted toes/fingers, missing at birth, deformed, bandaged, scars, etc., in the appropriate finger block(s).

NOTE:	FBI APPROVED "RETABS" CAN BE APPLIED TO ALL FINGER BLOCKS ON A FINGERPRINT CARD IF NECESSARY, WITH A LIMIT OF TWO (2) "RETABS" PER BLOCK.

CAUTION: Single Source State

If the card does not reflect your state bureau identification stamp when required, it will be returned immediately to the state bureau/submitting agency. Check with your state repository to determine if you are a single source state.

NOTE:	AT THIS POINT, A QUALITY REVIEW OF ARREST AND PERSONAL DESCRIPTOR DATA IS EXTERMELY IMPORTANT. THIS STEP CAN IMPROE THE QUALITY OF THE SUBMISSION AND HELP ELIMINATE IMMEDIATE REJECTS (CARDS RETURNED BY THE FBI WITHOUT ANY PROCESSING).

LEAVE BLANK

TYPE OR PRINT ALL INFORMATION IN BLACK

LEAVE BLANK

1

2

3   4

5

6   7 8   9 10 11 12   13

19   20   14

21   15

MNU 16

22   17

18

23

DATA ENTERED ON PALMPRINT CARDS

*This information is provided by the Latent Fingerprint Section at FBI Headquarters. Data fields preceded by an asterisk (*) must be completed.

Separate cards are required for each hand (FD 884)

See figure 4-7 on page 23-26 for an example of a Palmprint Cards (FD-884/884a)

1.   **Local Agency Identification/Reference (LIR) Number Block**

Enter your agency's identification or case number for the subject. The identification number must not exceed twenty (20) characters.

> NOTE: **THE PALMPRINT CARD IS A SUPPLEMENT TO THE CRIMINAL OR CIVIL FINGERPRINT CARD. PALMPRINT CARDS ARE NOT INTENDED TO STAND ALONE FROM THE ACTUAL FINGERPRINT CARD. THE PURPOSE OF THE PALMPRINT CARD SUPPLY PROVIDED TO STATE AND LOCAL AGENCIES IS TO ENCOURAGE THE RECORDING OF PALMPRINTS IN SUPPORT OF SOLVING MORE CRIMES THROUGH LATENT PRINT IDENTIFICATION AND TO PROVIDE A STANDARD FORMAT AS A BASIS FOR DEVELOPING AUTOMATED PALMPRINT SYSTEMS. THESE RECORDS SHOULD BE MAINTAINED AT THE LOCAL LEVEL.**

2.   ***Name (NAM) Block**

Enter the name obtained from the subject in this field. Abbreviations are **not** to be used for any part of the name. This format is last name followed by a comma (,) first and middle name, if any. Suffixes denoting seniority (Jr., Sr., III, etc.) should follow the middle or first name. Do not obstruct this area by using stamps, labels, holes or staples where the name has been printed.

3.   **State Identification Number (SID) Block**

Enter the SID when known. Enter SID numbers with no more than ten (10) alphanumeric characters, which includes the state abbreviation (i.e. NYXXXXXXXX). If labels are used for SID numbers, ensure the label used is an appropriate size for the SID block. **When the SID number is missing from a National Fingerprint (NFF) participant, the card will be rejected.**

4.   **FBI Number (FBI) Block**

Enter the assigned FBI number for the subject, if known.

5. ***Date Printed Block**

   Enter the date the subject was printed in month, day, and year format (i.e. MM/DD/YYYY).

6. ***Signature of Official Taking Palmprints**

   Enter the signature or name of the official taking prints. Also, list the official's ID number if applicable.

7. ***Originating Agency Identifier (ORI) Block**

   Enter your ORI number. Each agency is assigned its own unique ORI number. If you do not have an ORI number, you can contact your NCIC Control Terminal Officer (CTO) and an ORI number will be assigned to your agency. Federal agencies should contact their Federal Service Coordinator to obtain an ORI number.

8. *** Recording Side of Palmprint Block**

   This area is designed for recording the subject's right or left writer's palm (side) impression.

9. *** Recording Index Finger Block**

   This area is designated for recording the subject's right or left index finger if present. State which finger is printed (right or left).

10. ***Recording Palmprint Block**

    This area is designated for recording the subject's right or left palmprint. The hand symbols depict the direction the palmprints should be recorded on the card.

11. **Recording Rolled Fingerprint Impressions Block**

    It is very important that care be taken to roll the fingers from nail to nail when taking the individual finger impressions. This will help ensure legibility. Roll the print in the correct sequence. Indicate amputated fingers, tip-amputated, transplanted toes/fingers, missing at birth, deformed, bandaged, scars, etc., in the appropriate finger block(s).

12. **Additional Fingerprint/Palmprint Impressions Block**

    This area allows for the recording of additional fingerprint and/or palmprint impressions.

DATA ENTERED ON PALMPRINT CARDS

*This information is provided by the Latent Fingerprint Section at FBI Headquarters. Data fields preceded by an asterisk (*) must be completed.

Separate cards are required for each hand (FD 884a)

1. **Local Agency Identification/Reference (LIR) Number Block**

   Enter your agency's identification or case number for the subject. The identification number must not exceed twenty (20) characters.

2. ***Name (NAM) Block**

   Enter the name obtained from the subject in this field. Abbreviations are **not** to be used for any part of the name. This format is last name followed by a comma (,) first and middle name, if any. Suffixes denoting seniority (Jr., Sr., III, etc.) should follow the middle or first name. **Do not obstruct this area by using stamps, labels, holes or staples where the name has been printed.**

3. **State Identification Number (SID) Block**

   Enter the SID when known. Enter SID numbers with no more than ten (10) alphanumeric characters, which includes the state abbreviations (i.e. NYXXXXXXXX). If labels are used for SID numbers, ensure the label used is an appropriate size for the SID block. **When the SID number is missing from a National Fingerprint File (NFF) participant, the card will be rejected.**

4. **FBI Number (FBI) Block**

   Enter the assigned FBI number for the subject, if known.

5. ***Date printed Block**

   Enter the date the subject was printed in month, day, and year format (i.e. MM/DD/YYYY).

6. ***Signature of Official Taking Prints Block**

   Enter the signature or name of the official taking palmprints. Also list the official's ID number if applicable.

7. ***Originating Agency Identifier (ORI) Block**

Enter your ORI number. Each agency is assigned its own unique ORI number. If you do not have an ORI number, you can contact your NCIC Control Terminal Officer (CTO) and an ORI number will be assigned to your agency. Federal agencies should contact their Federal Service Coordinator to obtain an ORI number.

8. ***Hand Being Printed Block**

Check box to indicate hand being printed. **This should be the same hand as on the back of the card.**

9. *** Recording Index Finger Tip Block**

This area is designated for recording the subject's index finger tip - if present.

10. *** Recording Index Finger Rolled Impressions Block**

This area is designated for recording the index finger rolled impression – if present. It is very important that care be taken to roll the fingers from nail to nail when taking the individual finger impressions.

11. ***Recording Thumb Tip Block**

This area is designated for recording the subject's thumb tip - if present.

12. ***Recording Thumb Rolled Impression Block**

This area is designated for recording the thumb rolled impression – if present. It is very important that care be taken to roll the fingers from nail to nail when taking the individual finger impressions.

13. ***Recording Thenar Impressions Block**

This area is designated for recording the Thenar portion of the hand. Photo on card indicates area to be printed.

14. ***Hand Being Printed Block**

Check box for hand being printed. **This should be the same hand as on the front of the card.**

15. ***Recording Little Finger Tip Block**

This area is designated for recording the little finger tip – if present.

16. ***Recording Little Finger Rolled Impression Block**

This area is designated for recording the little finger rolled impression – if present. It is very important that care be taken to roll the fingers from nail to nail when taking the individual finger impressions.

17. ***Recording Middle Finger Tip Block**

This area is designated for recording the middle finger tip – if present.

18. ***Recording Middle Finger Rolled Impression Block**

This area is designated for recording the middle finger rolled impression – if present. It is very important that care be taken to roll the fingers from nail to nail when taking the individual finger impressions.

19. ***Recording Ring Finger Tip Block**

This area is designated for recording the ring finger tip – if present.

20. ***Recording Middle Ring Rolled Impression Block**

This area is designated for recording the ring finger rolled impression – if present. It is very important that care be taken to roll the fingers from nail to nail when taking the individual finger impressions.

☐ LEFT   8

☐ RIGHT

9

10

THUMB TIP

11

INDEX TIP

THUMB

INDEX

12

THENAR

13

Ball of Palm from One Hand

or

FD-884a (5-07-07) FEDERAL BUREAU OF INVESTIGATION, UNITED STATES DEPARTMENT OF JUSTICE, 26306

☐ LEFT

☐ RIGHT 14

15

16

17

MIDDLE TIP

LITTLE TIP

LITTLE

18

MIDDLE

RING TIP

19

RING 20

24

IDENTIFICATION NO.		LAST NAME		FIRST NAME	MIDDLE NAME	FBI NUMBER		TEL. NUMBER	
1			2				3		4

DATE PRINTED		SIGNATURE OF OFFICIAL TAKING PRINTS			ID NUMBER	CONTRIBUTOR (ORI)		
	5		6				7	

RIGHT FOUR FINGERS TAKEN SIMULTANEOUSLY		LEFT THUMB	RIGHT THUMB
8			
			9

10			

12

THUMB	INDEX	MIDDLE	RING	LITTLE
11				

REQUIRED FIELDS –DISPOSITION REPORT (R-84)

If any of the required fields are left blank, the R-84 will be rejected without further processing unless there is a quoted FBI Number.

Every effort should be made to enter the appropriate data in all fields (blocks) as shown on the Form R-84. Submitting complete information in all fields will eliminate delays and result in timely updates to Criminal History Records.

Name (NAM)

Date of Birth (DOB)

Contributor of Fingerprints

Date Arrested or Received

Offenses Charged at Arrest

Disposition Including Amended Charges

Submitting Agency

All data entered on fingerprint cards must be typewritten or legibly printed utilizing black or blue ink and must not exceed the boundaries of the designated field (block).

DATA SUBMITTED ON A DISPOSITION REPORT (R-84)

See Figure 8 on page 30 for an example of a Final Disposition Report (R-84)

Data fields preceded by an asterisk (*) must be completed in order for the Disposition Report to be processed by the FBI. However, all data fields are important and should be completed if the information is known.

1. **FBI Number**

    Enter the assigned FBI number for the subject, if known.

2. ***Name Block**

    Enter the subjects name given at the time of arrest. Abbreviations are not to be used for any part of the name. This format is last name followed by a comma (,) first and middle, if any. Suffixes denoting seniority (Jr., Sr., III, etc.) follow the middle or first name

3. ***Date of Birth (DOB)**

    Enter the DOB in month, day, and year format (i.e. MM/DD/YYYY). If a complete DOB is not known, enter the approximate age followed by the statement "YEARS OF AGE". **Disposition reports of persons 99 years old or older are not processed by the FBI; they will be rejected immediately**

4. **Sex**

    Sex must be indicated by either "F" (female) or "M" (male). See Sex Code Table on page 37 for additional codes.

5. **State Identification Number (SID)**

    Enter the State Identification Number (SID) when known. Enter SID number with no more than ten (10) alphanumeric characters, which includes the state abbreviation (i.e. NYXXXXXXXX).

6. **Social Security Number (SOC)**

    Enter the subject's Social Security number, if known. Additional Social Security numbers used by the subject may be entered on the back of the form.

7. ***Contributor of Fingerprints**

    Enter the name and location of the agency that submitted the original arrest fingerprint card.

8. **Arrest Number/Local Agency Identification Reference (OCA/LIR)**

    Enter the arresting agency's Local identification Number (OCA/LIR) or case number for the subject. The OCA/LIR must not exceed twenty (20) characters.

9. ***Date Arrested or Received**

    Enter the date the subject was arrested by the submitter of the original arrest fingerprint card in month, day, and year (i.e. MM/DD/YYYY).

10. ***Offenses Charged at Arrest**

    Enter the original arrest charge(s) in literal terms; (i.e. murder, rape, robbery, assault). Numeric four digit NCIC Codes cannot be used. State or local citation numbers may be listed but a literal should be listed also. If federal citations numbers are listed a literal should be listed also. Charge literals are important for those using the Criminal History Record for licensing employment suitability determination and agencies that do not have access to all citation numbers that may be used.

    If more room is needed, additional charges may be entered in the blank area on the back of the form. Number each charge to correspond with the disposition information.

11. *** Disposition and Date**

    Enter dispositional information, including the sentence date. Indicate the type of sentence imposed if applicable (i.e. consecutive, concurrent, probation) numbering to correspond with the appropriate charge. If the subject was convicted or plead guilty to a lesser charge, include the modification. **If a single disposition applies to all charges listed, please indicate that;** (i.e. 5 yrs on charge of burglary and theft). **It is not necessary to list "Disposition not available", "Not yet disposed" or any similar phrase.** If additional room is needed, use the blank space on the back of the form.

12. ***This form Submitted By:**

    Enter the ORI number, agency, city and state of the submitter. On appropriate lines provide signature, date, and title.

13. **Court Ordered Expungement**

    If a certified copy of a court ordered expungement is submitted, place a check mark in the box to the left of "COURT ORDERED EXPUNGEMENT". Staple the court order to the Final Disposition Report (R-84).

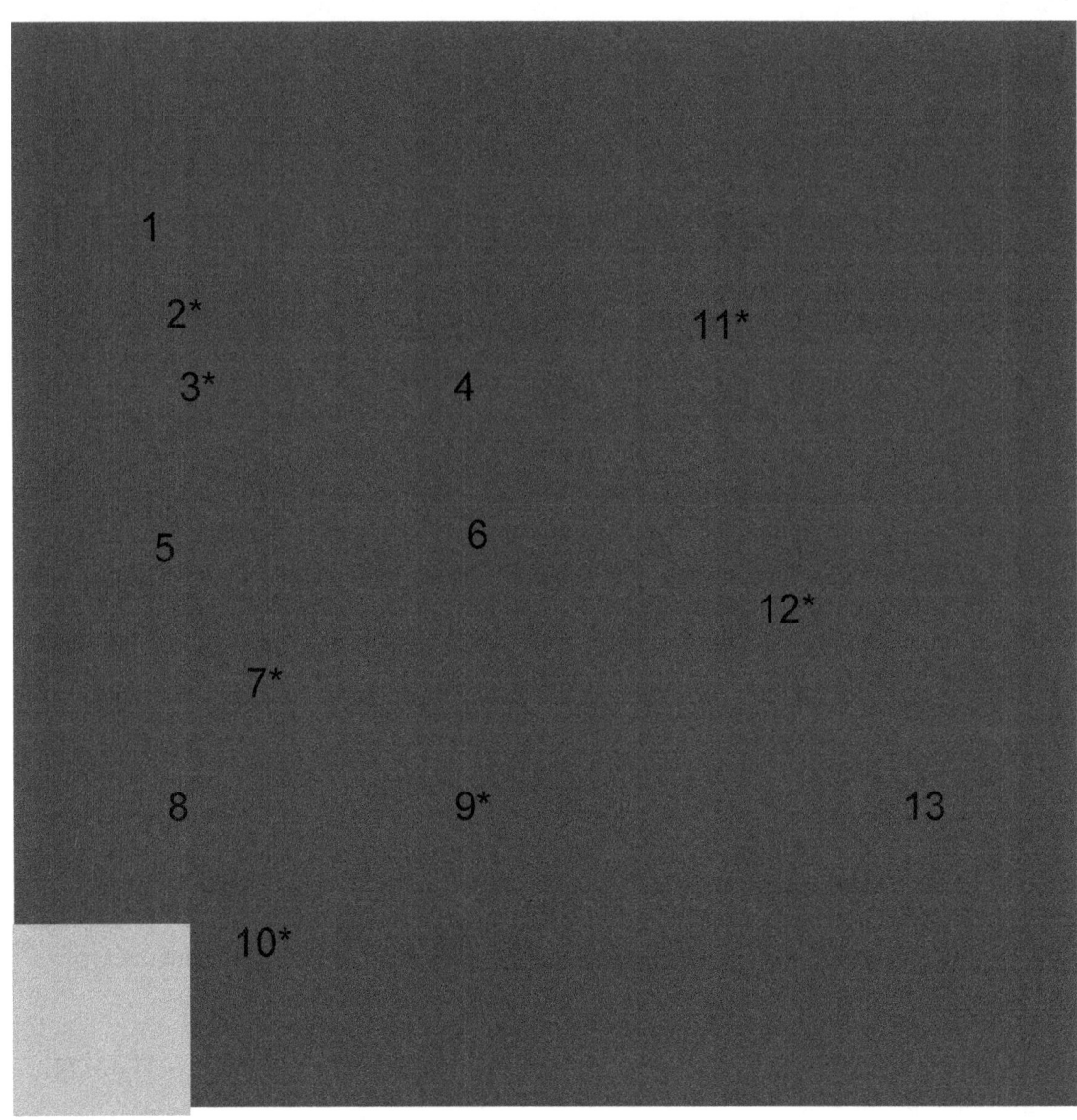

REQUIRED FIELDS – FLASH/CANCELLATION NOTICE (I-12)

If any of the required fields are left blank, the Flash/Cancellation Notice (I-12) will be rejected without further processing unless there is a quoted FBI Number.

Every effort should be made to enter the appropriate data in all fields (blocks) as shown on the Form I-12. Submitting complete information in all fields will eliminate delays and result in timely updates to the Criminal History Records.

Fill in Cancel Block if I-12 is a Flash Cancellation

Name (NAM)
Date of Birth (DOB)
Flash Information
Final Disposition
Offense
FBI Number
Agency to be Notified of Apprehension

DATA SUBMITTED ON FLASH/CANCLELLATION FORM (I-12)

See Figure 9 on page 36 for an example of a Flash/Cancellation Form (I-12)

Data fields preceded by an asterisk (*) must be completed in order for the Flash/Cancellation Form to be processed by the FBI. However, all data fields are important and should be completed if the information is known.

1. **Date**

    Enter the current date.

2. ***Flash Block (This is not required when submitting a cancellation notice).**

    Enter the supervision beginning date(s) and ending date(s) in month, day and year format (i.e. MM/DD/YYYY). The time period entered and the type of supervision must match the information provided in the "Final Disposition" block #4.

3. **Date and Place of Sentence Block**

    Enter the date sentencing took place, in month, day and year format i.e. MM/DD/YYYY). Enter the city and state where sentencing took place.

4. ***Final Disposition Block**

    Enter the period of incarceration, suspended sentence, fines, and period of supervision. The time period entered and the type of supervision must match the information provided in the "Flash" block #2.

5. **Charge Blocks**

    Enter the charge(s) in literal terms (i.e. murder, rape, robbery, assault, etc.). Numeric four digit NCIC Codes and U.S. Title Codes cannot be used alone, but may be included in the literal charge.

    If citation numbers are shown without literals, the form will be rejected without being processed. If more room is needed., additional charges may be entered in the blank area on the back of the form.

6. **Contributor of Fingerprints Block**

    Enter the name and location of the agency that submitted the original fingerprint card.

7. *Cancel Block

A prompt notification is requested when the subject's supervision is terminated, set aside, or revoked. The effective date must also be included.

8. *Name Block

Enter the most complete name available for the subject. Abbreviations are not to be used for any part of the name. The format is last name, followed by a comma (,) first and middle name, if any. Suffixes denoting seniority (Jr., Sr., III, etc.) should follow the middle or first name.

9. Residence Block

Enter the complete residential address of the subject, if known.

10. Aliases Block

List other names used by the subject that are different than the name entered in "NAM" block #8, including signature name, using the same format (i.e. LAST, FIRST, MIDDLE, SUFFIX).

11. Numbers Blocks

Arrest -	Enter arrest (OCA/LIR) or prison number assigned by the arresting/receiving agency, if known.
Military -	Enter the subject's military service number, if known.
Alien -	Enter the subject's assigned Alien Registration number, if known.
Social Security -	Enter the subject's Social Security Number, if known, and any additional Social Security Numbers used.

12. Occupation Block

List the subject's occupation, if available.

13. Race Block

Indicate subject's race using the Race Code Chart on page 40.

14. **Sex Block**

Sex must be indicated by either "F" (female) or "M" (male). See Sex Code Chart on page 37 for additional codes.

15. **Height Block**

Height must be expressed in feet and inches. Fractions of an inch should be rounded off. Inches less than ten should be preceded by a zero. For example, five feet four inches should be submitted as "504", and six feet even should be submitted as "600".

16. **Citizenship Block**

Enter "U.S." if the subject is a citizen of the United States; otherwise, enter the appropriate country. Use the correct abbreviation for foreign countries or correctly spell the name of the country. A list of approved abbreviations can be found in the NCIC manual. "Yes" or "No" responses are not acceptable.

17. **Weight Block**

Weight must be expressed in pounds. Fractions of a pound should be rounded off to the nearest pound.

18. **Eye Color Block**

Enter the subject's eye color by entering one of the three-character codes on page 37.

19. **Hair Color Block**

Enter the subject's hair color by entering one of the three-character codes on page 38.

20. ***FBI Number Block**

Enter the assigned FBI number for the subject. If the FBI number is not entered, the form will be automatically rejected without processing. *Refer to back side of Form I-12, figure 9, for specific instructions.

21. ***Date of Birth Block**

Enter the DOB in month, day and year format (i.e. MM/DD/YYYY). If a complete DOB is not known, enter the approximate age followed by the statement "YEARS OF AGE". **Flash/Cancellation Notices of persons 99 years old or older are not processed by the FBI; they will be rejected immediately**.

22. **Place of Birth Block**

List the subject's state, territorial possession, province (Canadian), or country of birth. Use the correct abbreviation for foreign countries or correctly spell the name of the country. A list of approved abbreviations can be found in the *NCIC Code Manual*. **Do not list a county as a POB.**

23. **Scars, Marks, Tattoos, and Amputations block**

List any scars, marks, tattoos, discolorations, moles, missing or artificial body parts, deformities, piercings, needle marks, transplanted toes/fingers, and/or amputations.

24. **Agency Case or File Number Block**

Enter the number assigned by the supervising agency.

25. **Please Furnish Identification Block**

To request a copy of the subject's Criminal History Record, at the time the flash is being posted, place a check mark in the box provided.

26. **Agency, *ORI Number and Address of Parties to be Notified of Subjects Apprehension**

List the agency to be notified if the subject incurs any additional criminal arrests during the supervision period.

27. **Agency, *ORI Number, and Address of Contributor**

Enter the Originating Agency Identifier (ORI) number, agency, and address of the contributor submitting the form.

To order any of the forms discussed in this guide (free of charge) or for questions concerning your supply order, contact the FBI at (304) 625-3983. Orders can be submitted electronically at www.fbi.govhq/cjisd/forms/orderingfps.htm. Orders using Form I-178 (See page 43 may be sent by facsimile to (304) 625-3984 or by mailing to:

Federal Bureau of Investigation
CJIS Division
Attn: Logistical Support Unit
1000 Custer Hollow Road
Clarksburg, WV 26306

Flash/Cancellation Notice
1-12 (Rev. 9-28-99)

Date _____ 1

To: FBI, CJS Division
     Clarksburg, WV 26306

	(date)		(date)		(date)		(date)
Flash: Mandatory Release	_____	Expires	_____	Parole	_____	Expires	_____
2* Supervised Release	_____	Expires	_____	SPT	_____	Expires	_____
Probation	_____	Expires	_____	PTD	_____	Expires	_____

When requesting flash notice, give the following information:

Date and Place of Sentence 3	Final Disposition 4*
Charge 5*	

Contributor of Fingerprints   6

☐ CANCEL (reason)   7*

Name 8*	Residence 9

Aliases	Numbers	Occupation
	Arrest 11	12

	Military 11	Race 13	Sex 14	Height 15	Citizenship 16

FBI#* 20*	Alien 11	Weight 17	Eyes 18	Hair 19	

Date of Birth 21*	Social Security 11	

Place of Birth 22	Scars, marks and tattoos 23

Agency Case or File Number 24	☐ Please Furnish Identification Record 25

Agency *ORI#, and Address of Parties to be notified of Apprehension: 26*	Agency, *ORI#, and Address of Contributor 27*

*FBI# and ORI# Must be indicated or form will be returned without being processed.
See over for Instructions

SEX CODE TABLE

External Code	Literal	Description
F	Female	Female
G	Female	Female Print, Male Reference
M	Male	Male
N	Male	Male Print, Female Reference
Y	Male	Male, Unreported
Z	Female	Female, Unreported
X	Unknown	Unknown Sex

EYE COLOR CODE TABLE

Eye Color Literal	External Code
BLACK	BLK
BLUE	BLU
BROWN	BRO
GRAY	GRY
GREEN	GRN
HAZEL	HAZ
MAROON	MAR

HAIR CODE TABLE

BALD	BLD
BLACK	BLK
BLONDE (or strawberry)	BLN
BLUE	BLU
BROWN	BRO
GREEN	GRN
GRAY (or partially gray)	GRY
ORANGE	ONG
PURPLE	PLE
PINK	PNK
RED (or auburn)	RED
SANDY	SDY
WHITE	WHI
UNKNOWN	XXX

RACE CODE TABLE

External Code	Literal	Description (If Subject Is)
A	Asian or Pacific Islander	Chinese, Japanese, Filipino, Korean, Polynesian, Indian, Indonesian, Asian Indian, Samoan, or other Pacific Islander
B	Black	A person having origins in any of the black racial groups of Africa
I	American Indian or Alaskan Native	American Indian, Eskimo, or Alaskan Native, or a person having origins in any of the 48 contiguous states of the United States or Alaska who maintains cultural identification through tribal affiliation or community recognition
U	Unknown	Of Indeterminable Race
W	White	Caucasian, Mexican, Puerto Rican, Cuban, Central or South American, or other Spanish culture or origin, regardless of race.

MNU PREFIX CODES

External Code	Description
AF	Air Force Serial Number
AN	Non-Immigrant Admission Number
AR	Alien Registration Number
AS	Army Serial Number (including National Guard and Air National Guard)
BF	Bureau Fugitive
CI	Canadian Social Insurance Number
CG	U.S. Coast Guard Serial Number
IO	Identification Order Number
MD	Mariner's Document or Identification Number
MC	Marine Corps Serial Number
MP	Royal Canadian Mounted Police Identification Number (FPS Number)
NA	National Agency Case Number – Military
NS	Navy Serial Number
OA	Originating Agency Police Identification Number
PI	Personal Identification Number (State Issued only)
PP	Passport Number
PS	Port Security Card Number
SS	Selective Service Number
VA	Veterans Administration Claim Number

Telephone Contacts

*WEST VIRGINIA CJIS COMPLEX SWITCHBOARD
Phone 304-625-2000

*IAFIS USER SUPPORT (HELP DESK) - Centralized problem reporting, tracking, and monitoring.
Phone 304-625-4357

*SPECIAL PROCESSING CENTER - Processes criminal expedite fingerprint and special record services requests. Example: a request from law enforcement that requires immediate attention. Operates 24 hours a day, 7 days a week.
Phone: 304-625-5584 Fax: 304-625-5587

*ANSWER HITS TO WANTS GROUP – Places/removes wanted person information, parole/probation flags.
Phone: 304-625-4618 Fax: 304-625-4557

*CORRESPONDENCE GROUP – Handles information regarding congressional matters and requests that originate through the Freedom of Information Act. Example: individuals who request a copy of their own record for private use.
Phone: 304-625-3878 Fax: 304-625-3571

*CUSTOMER SERVICE GROUP – Serves local, state, and federal law enforcement agencies and private citizens dealing with matters of a complex nature regarding the acceptance, processing, and dissemination of fingerprint card submissions to the CJIS Division. This group serves as the point of contact for numerous agencies to resolve specific problems involving excessing processing time for civil applicant fingerprint card submissions and other concerns. This group also provides explanations of FBI policies and procedures to law enforcement agencies and individuals regarding the various services provided by the CJIS Division
Phone 304-625-5590 Fax 304-625-3571